#SCRUM tweet

140 Thought-Lenses to Build Better Software Using Scrum

Utpal Vaishnav

Foreword by Jesse Fewell

An Actionable Business Journal

E-mail: info@thinkaha.com
20660 Stevens Creek Blvd., Suite 210
Cupertino, CA 95014

Published by THiNKaha®
20660 Stevens Creek Blvd., Suite 210, Cupertino, CA 95014
http://thinkaha.com
E-mail: info@thinkaha.com

First Printing: October 2016
Paperback ISBN: 978-1-61699-110-4 (1-61699-110-0)
eBook ISBN: 978-1-61699-111-1 (1-61699-111-9)
Place of Publication: Silicon Valley, California, USA
Paperback Library of Congress Number: 2012953746

Trademarks

All terms mentioned in this book that are known to be trademarks or service marks have been appropriately capitalized. Neither THiNKaha, nor any of its imprints, can attest to the accuracy of this information. Use of a term in this book should not be regarded as affecting the validity of any trademark or service mark.

Warning and Disclaimer

Every effort has been made to make this book as complete and as accurate as possible. The information provided is on an "as is" basis. The author(s), publisher, and their agents assume no responsibility for errors or omissions. Nor do they assume liability or responsibility to any person or entity with respect to any loss or damages arising from the use of information contained herein.

Advance Praises

"*#SCRUM tweet* is full of practical wisdom on Scrum, both as a powerful execution methodology and as a mindset. These insights will certainly help your team in simplifying work, increasing focus, and delivering better outcomes. Read, adapt these lessons to your context, and you will get more done—qualitatively!"
Tanmay Vora (@tnvora), Author/Blogger/Social Media Influencer, Founder of http://QAspire.com, and Director (R&D) at Basware Corporation

"There are a lot of very nice and well-phrased tweets, very well done!"
Mikael Fagerholm, Head of Development at Aditro

"Utpal Vaishnav has been there and done that. This book includes excellent questions, which hopefully make everybody implementing Scrum projects to stop and think. That will help to avoid mistakes and save time and money."
Pentti Heikkinen, CEO and Founder of Gateway Technolabs Finland Oy

Dedication

This book is dedicated to you, the reader, for believing that it can help you take your Scrum knowledge to the next level. Be a part of the difference by using Scrum.

Acknowledgments

Thanks to Twitter for the 140-character constraint that provided me an opportunity to be precise and on target.

Thanks to my friend and mentor, Rajesh Setty (@RajSetty), for guiding and encouraging me to write.

Thanks to my friend, Tanmay Vora (@tnvora), for writing #QUALITYtweet[1] and inspiring me to write a THiNKaha book.

Thanks to Gateway Technolabs and Aditro for providing me ample opportunities to take my Scrum skills to the next level.

Thanks to Diane Vo, production manager at THiNKaha, for working with me on the book production process.

Thanks to my publisher, Mitchell Levy (@HappyAbout), for taking on my first book.

Heartfelt thanks to my wife, Kavita Vaishnav (@kavutpal), for her kind support. The time invested to create this book is taken from her time. I owe it to her.

Special thanks to my parents, especially to my father, who inspired me in his unique ways to live an agile life.

1. Tanmay Vora, *#QUALITYtweet: 140 Bite-Sized Ideas to Deliver Quality in Every Project* (Cupertino, CA: THiNKaha, 2009).

Why I Wrote This Book

It is no longer news that agile software development frameworks are taking over the software development world.

The reason is simple: agile frameworks offer more human-friendly approaches that ensure quicker results.

The art of simplifying and limiting works-in-progress is at the core of most agile frameworks. Twitter, one of the most successful micro-blogging platforms, is known for its simplicity and constraint of 140-character tweets. That is where Twitter and agile thinking intersects.

People want to read, learn, and grow faster than ever. They often have little time to invest for reading and learning from long articles and books.

I wrote *#SCRUM tweet* as a solution for people who want to build great software using Scrum.

Read, share, and create software that matters!

All the best!

Utpal Vaishnav

Twitter: [@utpalvaishnav](#)

How to Read a THiNKaha® Book
A Note from the Publisher

The THiNKaha series is the CliffsNotes of the 21st century. The value of these books is that they are contextual in nature. Although the actual words won't change, their meaning will change every time you read one as your context will change. Experience your own "AHA!" moments ("AHAmessages™") with a THiNKaha book; AHAmessages are looked at as "actionable" moments—think of a specific project you're working on, an event, a sales deal, a personal issue, etc. and see how the AHAmessages in this book can inspire your own AHAmessages, something that you can specifically act on. Here's how to read one of these books and have it work for you:

1. Read a THiNKaha book (these slim and handy books should only take about 15–20 minutes of your time!) and write down one to three actionable items you thought of while reading it. Each journal-style THiNKaha book is equipped with space for you to write down your notes and thoughts underneath each AHAmessage.

2. Mark your calendar to re-read this book again in 30 days.

3. Repeat step #1 and write down one to three more AHAmessages that grab you this time. I guarantee that they will be different than the first time. BTW: this is also a great time to reflect on the actions taken from the last set of AHAmessages you wrote down.

After reading a THiNKaha book, writing down your AHAmessages, re-reading it, and writing down more AHAmessages, you'll begin to see how these books contextually apply to you. THiNKaha books advocate for continuous, lifelong learning. They will help you transform your AHAs into actionable items with tangible results until you no longer have to say "AHA!" to these moments—they'll become part of your daily practice as you continue to grow and learn.

As the Chief Instigator of AHAs at THiNKaha, I definitely practice what I preach. I read *Alexisms* and *Ted Rubin on How to Look People in the Eye Digitally*, and one new book once a month and take away two to three different action items from each of them every time. Please e-mail me your AHAs today!

Mitchell Levy
publisher@thinkaha.com

Contents

Foreword by Jesse Fewell

Utpal has a voice, and you will be enriched for listening.

In the months and years since we first met in Scrum class, he has built an ever-growing body of perspectives and thoughts on delivering great products, particularly on using agile techniques like Scrum. However, you may not have noticed, because he's delivered his thoughts as a steady, prolific stream of tweets and posts, one thought at a time. Unlike conventional thought leaders who publish years of study all at once in print, Utpal has walked the talk: broadcasting small increments of wisdom, one tweet at a time, very much in the spirit of Scrum.

I'm also delighted by the idea of this book, re-delivering a proven product to a broader audience. What worked well in a digital medium works really well in this compact print format. Heck, you could use it to continue the learning cycle. Try kicking off a retrospective meeting by reading off one of these ahas from the book:

"What the traditional project manager cures, the ScrumMaster prevents." (Aha #62)

"The rate at which you deliver should be faster than the rate at which the product expectations change." (Aha #13)

"There's no such thing as boring projects. There are only boring team members." (Aha #69)

These and many other gems are in the pages that follow, containing both his own original quotes, as well as reprises of other great agile quotes.

Jesse Fewell
Writer, Speaker, Coach

Section I

Build the Right Mindset

Scrum teams are comprised of people who, if not nurtured carefully, can turn into your chief impediments on the journey to building great software. The attitude of your team and their alignment to the product vision are the two most important factors for building successful software with Scrum. This section offers practical thought-lenses on building and nurturing the right mindset and how it can impact the overall success of a software delivery.

1

Critical question: What's the point of creating a "perfect" software that never ships? @utpalvaishnav

_____

_____

_____

2

What does your software framework deliver
quickly? Project status or the product?
@utpalvaishnav

_____

_____

_____

3

No processes or certifications can help
build great software if you staff your project
with mediocre team members.
@utpalvaishnav

_____

_____

_____

4

Top two reasons for poor software:
1) People don't know what matters;
2) They don't know the means to get
what matters done. @utpalvaishnav

_____

_____

_____

5

Your product development is like your
heart. If you don't take care of it, you'll get a
heart attack. @utpalvaishnav

_____

_____

_____

6

If you base your rewards on meeting deadlines, people might meet them with inferior quality software. @utpalvaishnav

_____

_____

_____

7

Two great misfortunes in any project: not knowing the impediments and not resolving those impediments in a timely manner. @utpalvaishnav

_____

_____

_____

8

"Great software" is a judgment your customers will make, not you.
@utpalvaishnav

_____

_____

_____

9

Handle your methodologies as just a means to deliver. Historically, they have a tendency to take a lead. @utpalvaishnav

_____

_____

_____

10

In Scrum, people don't need permission to think for themselves. @utpalvaishnav

_____

_____

_____

11

People who haven't failed haven't really created software before. @utpalvaishnav

_____

_____

_____

12

Does your project management system REALLY help you build high-performance software faster? @utpalvaishnav

_____

_____

_____

13

The rate at which you deliver should be faster than the rate at which the product expectations change. @utpalvaishnav

---

14

The first step of building great software is to know WHY that software product NEEDS to be great. @utpalvaishnav

15

Have disengaged, demotivated teams that don't collaborate much and lack trust? Huh, are you using Scrum correctly?
@utpalvaishnav

_____

_____

_____

16

Scrum is not about using different techniques; it is about leveraging techniques differently. @utpalvaishnav

_____

_____

_____

17

You should determine ideal sprint length based on iterations and interactions.
It's not what is given as a "2-4 week rule."
@utpalvaishnav

_____

_____

_____

18

Learned the lessons? Apply it in the next sprint. Now that's what matters.
@utpalvaishnav

_____

_____

_____

19

In Scrum, the most important thing is to keep the most important thing the most important thing. @utpalvaishnav

_____

_____

_____

20

Scrum will let you navigate without a map. It's like a compass that enables you to find the true north. @utpalvaishnav

_____

_____

_____

21

The goal is to do the right kind of work, not to eliminate re-work. Re-work is fine if it is the right kind. @utpalvaishnav

_____

_____

_____

22

The core of Scrum is having a surefooted ScrumMaster who realizes that caring doesn't equate weakness. @utpalvaishnav

_____

_____

_____

23

The pursuit of Scrum is not about getting it done. It's about getting it done the best way you can. @utpalvaishnav

_____

_____

_____

24

There's no such thing as Scrum compliance.
A Scrum team just makes it happen.
@utpalvaishnav

_____

_____

_____

25

Scrum team members often choose to laugh
at themselves. @utpalvaishnav

_____

_____

_____

26

The trust you implant in your Scrum team
is proportional to the consistency of results
the team produces. @utpalvaishnav

_____

_____

_____

27

Stakeholders of a Scrum project understand
that an estimate is not commitment.
@utpalvaishnav

_____

_____

_____

28

Primary measure of progress in Scrum: customers obtaining value from continuous delivery. @utpalvaishnav

_____

_____

_____

29

No sustainable pace, no long-term agility. @utpalvaishnav

_____

_____

_____

30

Roles, ceremonies, and artifacts are the
most important elements, but Scrum is
more than the sum of them. @utpalvaishnav

_____

_____

_____

31

If you spent more than an hour preparing for a sprint review, you've done something wrong. @utpalvaishnav

_____

_____

_____

32

The most difficult thing about Scrum is that it is too simple. @utpalvaishnav

_____

_____

_____

33

Don't improve Scrum. Instead, improve your software that uses Scrum. @utpalvaishnav

_____

_____

_____

34

Improving a product is not a project.
It's an ongoing activity that doesn't have
an end date. @utpalvaishnav

_____

_____

_____

35

7 actions your Scrum team should take: list, prioritize, pick, commit, remove impediments, make sure it's done, and deliver. @utpalvaishnav

_____

_____

_____

36

Actions and outcomes versus planning and processes. Left is valued more than right in Scrum.[2] @utpalvaishnav

_____

_____

_____

---

2. Agile Manifesto, of which Scrum is based on, lists down left side and right side. Visit http://www.agilemanifesto.org/ for more information.

37

Don't get into Scrum if you don't get to see
what your customer is seeing.
@utpalvaishnav

_____

_____

_____

38

Condemn actions, not team members.
@utpalvaishnav

_____

_____

_____

39

Be adept at adapting. @utpalvaishnav

_____

_____

_____

40

Too much of anything is malignant.
Just enough of everything is benignant.
@utpalvaishnav

_____

_____

_____

41

Do more of what adds value. Do less of what does not. @utpalvaishnav

_____

_____

_____

42

Scrum is for you only if you know NO fear. Otherwise, you'll tend to pretend things are very "un-agile." @utpalvaishnav

_____

_____

_____

43

To implement Scrum correctly, you need to actively listen. You get increased self-awareness as a byproduct. @utpalvaishnav

_____

_____

_____

44

Scrum makes you more human-receptive rather than reactive. @utpalvaishnav

_____

_____

_____

45

If you don't want to practice work/life balance, Scrum is NOT for you. @utpalvaishnav

_____

_____

_____

46

When you work on two projects simultaneously, you give 50 percent of your attention to each. Scrum discourages that. @utpalvaishnav

_____

_____

_____

47

Understand basic principles of self-organization before trying to understand Scrum. @utpalvaishnav

_____

_____

_____

48

Product Backlog: The features that we don't prioritize may be infinite, but the features we prioritize have to be finite.
@utpalvaishnav

_____

_____

_____

49

Scrum in three words: learn, unlearn, re-learn. @utpalvaishnav

_____

_____

_____

Section II

Build the Great Software

The Scrum framework is the foundation upon which great software can be built. It is not a set of work instructions but rather, a facilitator that gradually builds high-performance software. Deep understanding of roles, ceremonies, and artifacts offered by Scrum are leveraged to deliver great software. This section presents ideas on how to effectively build high-performance software faster.

50

Great planning + poor execution = disaster.
Okay planning + great execution = success!
@utpalvaishnav

51

A Scrum project is like a recipe dish. The
recipe is as good as the chefs preparing it.
@utpalvaishnav

52

The recipe for great software: prioritized product backlog, self-organizing team, and a great ScrumMaster. @utpalvaishnav

_____

_____

_____

53

Get clear on "what matters," then commit to "how" you'll achieve it in daily Scrum and no one can keep you away from the sprint goals. @utpalvaishnav

_____

_____

_____

54

In order for change to happen, for good or bad, fear should be suppressed by actions. No actions, no results. @utpalvaishnav

_____

_____

_____

55

The secret of success in Scrum is reflecting, inspecting, and adapting quickly. Don't focus on doing everything right.
@utpalvaishnav

_____

_____

_____

56

The attitude of your Product Owner will determine the caliber of your software.
@utpalvaishnav

_____

_____

_____

57

The recent software feature you add is an assessment of your mission, values, and integrity as a business. @utpalvaishnav

_____

_____

_____

58

The ultimate illusion: expecting great
software from the team without defining
what great software looks like.
@utpalvaishnav

_____

_____

_____

59

Don't want to work closely with the team?
Find any role aside from the Product
Owner. @utpalvaishnav

_____

_____

_____

60

If you assign more work to your Scrum team in the middle of a sprint, beware of inferior quality software. @utpalvaishnav

_____

_____

_____

61

The whole team is led by the vision of the Product Owner. Remember, that role is a great responsibility in itself. @utpalvaishnav

_____

_____

_____

62

What the traditional project manager cures, the ScrumMaster prevents. @utpalvaishnav

---

63

GOOD ScrumMasters work on a couple of projects. Great ScrumMasters work on only ONE. @utpalvaishnav

---

64

Have any of the team members under-delivered? That implies that the ScrumMaster didn't do a good job.
@utpalvaishnav

_____

_____

_____

65

Think you're a team manager? Well, you're not. A ScrumMaster is a facilitator who serves the team as a Scrum coach. @utpalvaishnav

---

66

How to measure a ScrumMaster's performance? Measure if the team won. (Easy, isn't it?) @utpalvaishnav

_____

_____

_____

67

A ScrumMaster is a change agent who develops a high-performing and continuously improving team that delivers value. @utpalvaishnav

_____

_____

_____

68

There are no rules for good Scrum teams;
there are only good Scrum teams.
@utpalvaishnav

_____

_____

_____

69

There's no such thing as boring projects.
There are only boring team members.
@utpalvaishnav

_____

_____

_____

70

Great software is a spin-off achieved by passionate people working toward the most important product goals. @utpalvaishnav

_____

_____

_____

71

Distressed, unorganized teams rarely make software that make customers happy. @utpalvaishnav

_____

_____

_____

72

In Scrum, delivery is owned by every team member, regardless of their titles.
@utpalvaishnav

_____

_____

_____

73

Implementing a software feature is much easier when the same people are involved in defining the same feature. @utpalvaishnav

---

74

People who always build great software invariably love what they do. @utpalvaishnav

---

75

People who are comfortable being uncomfortable are great candidates for a Scrum team. They make a difference. @utpalvaishnav

_____

_____

_____

76

Compliant engineers rarely build great
software. Risk takers do, but the risk has to
be the right kind. @utpalvaishnav

_____

_____

_____

77

Teams that let their software speak earn more respect and wealth. @utpalvaishnav

_____

_____

_____

78

The key to building a great Scrum team: realize that people need trust, time, and boosts to make a difference. @utpalvaishnav

_____

_____

_____

79

Have ability but no intent? Better find a
non-Scrum team. @utpalvaishnav

_____

_____

_____

80

Having a member on the team who doesn't produce any value is like NOT having that team member at all. @utpalvaishnav

_____

_____

_____

81

Be concerned with the software quality rather than how team members have spent their time delivering it. @utpalvaishnav

_____

_____

_____

82

Do you REALLY need to read the audit report when the software being built is EXACTLY as per the expectations? @utpalvaishnav

_____

_____

_____

83

If you don't know WHY you wrote that particular line of code, how will you be sure of a great quality software? @utpalvaishnav

_____

_____

_____

84

In Scrum, here's what matters more than theory: practice married with the art of things not done. @utpalvaishnav

_____

_____

_____

85

Building better software is like achieving a high score on a game. After each game, the bar is raised. @utpalvaishnav

_____

_____

_____

86

Great software is not just *desirable* anymore. It's the most basic need in today's competitive market. @utpalvaishnav

_____

_____

_____

87

Working on most important features and failing fast matters more than effectively delivering features that don't matter much. @utpalvaishnav

_____

_____

_____

88

Improving unimportant features is a
self-invited waste. Do whatever possible to
avoid that. @utpalvaishnav

89

You will not get all the benefits of Scrum
if you don't use it the right way.
@utpalvaishnav

90

Critical question: Does your Scrum project make it easy for your clients to work with you? @utpalvaishnav

_____

_____

_____

91

Integrity, trust, and over-communication married with the right skills determine the success of a Scrum project. @utpalvaishnav

_____

_____

_____

92

Quality in a Scrum project is achieved via over-communication and the right execution. @utpalvaishnav

---

93

Attention to detail is a trait that every Scrum team member should have. @utpalvaishnav

---

94

Don't regret a failed sprint. Learn from it and make it right next time. @utpalvaishnav

_____

_____

_____

95

The purpose of sprint is the sprint of purpose. @utpalvaishnav

_____

_____

_____

96

Be aware. Take actions. Have results.
@utpalvaishnav

_____

_____

_____

97

In Scrum, conflict is a tool that helps the
team make software better. @utpalvaishnav

_____

_____

_____

98

Successful software is not about what's in it but what's left out of it. Scrum ensures that. @utpalvaishnav

_____

_____

_____

99

Working software, and ONLY working software, matters to your end customers, not the processes or anything else. @utpalvaishnav

_____

_____

_____

100

If you're not busy collaborating with your customers, you're busy collaborating with potential failure. @utpalvaishnav

_____

_____

_____

101

Great engineering skills may not lead to the most useful software. Great understanding of customer needs will. @utpalvaishnav

_____

_____

_____

102

When it comes to building great software using Scrum, the benefits always supersede the features. @utpalvaishnav

_____

_____

_____

103

Only working software can justify the methodologies. And you thought it was the methodologies that mattered? @utpalvaishnav

104

Sometimes it's all about making a decision, right or wrong. @utpalvaishnav

Section III

Inspect and Adapt

The ability to inspect and adapt is the heart of
Scrum. This very ability helps you better deal
with subsequent uncertainties. Scrum is not about
methodology or techniques but about building
people's abilities to effortlessly align with changes.
This section presents ideas about how to align with
changing business needs without losing focus.

105

The ability to inspect and adapt is superior to years of experience. Each Scrum team member should have that. @utpalvaishnav

_____

_____

_____

106

Don't justify poor delivery. Instead, make it better next time. Inspect and adapt.
@utpalvaishnav

_____

_____

_____

107

Following the plan may have value.
Responding to change certainly has more.
@utpalvaishnav

_____

_____

_____

108

Right people + wrong tool = delayed success.
Wrong people + right tool = no success.
Better late than never. @utpalvaishnav

_____

_____

_____

109

Learn by experiencing. Improve by reflecting. @utpalvaishnav

_____

_____

_____

110

There are no wrong ways to do something RIGHT. @utpalvaishnav

_____

_____

_____

111

Override excuses with actions. The sooner, the better. @utpalvaishnav

_____

_____

_____

112

Don't tell your team members what the right thing to do is; ask questions that make them do it. @utpalvaishnav

_____

_____

_____

113

Know the product, know fellow team members, know yourself, and take the right actions—that's the key to success. @utpalvaishnav

_____

_____

_____

114

Every conquered impediment moves you ahead in the direction of what matters most. @utpalvaishnav

_____

_____

_____

115

The most difficult challenge for the ScrumMaster is dealing with lost self-confidence. @utpalvaishnav

_____

_____

_____

116

Like lunches, lessons learned aren't free.
Make every penny count. @utpalvaishnav

117

How to serve your team even if you can't
play? Simple. Get off the playground.
@utpalvaishnav

118

Doing something without knowing why is like eating without digesting. @utpalvaishnav

_____

_____

_____

119

The number one problem that keeps you away from success is inaction, not lack of skills. @utpalvaishnav

_____

_____

_____

120

Behaviors are mirrors of the mind; they reflect who you are. @utpalvaishnav

_____

_____

_____

121

Those who don't learn from past mistakes are doomed to repeat them. @utpalvaishnav

_____

_____

_____

122

Start something only when you are certain you'll finish it. @utpalvaishnav

_____

_____

_____

123

Of all the things you wear, your behavior is the most important. @utpalvaishnav

_____

_____

_____

124

Admitting your mistake is a modest way
of exhibiting that you've grown a little wiser.
@utpalvaishnav

_____

_____

_____

125

The only impediments you can resolve are
the ones you discern. @utpalvaishnav

_____

_____

_____

126

Rigidity and Scrum team members do not go together. @utpalvaishnav

_____

_____

_____

127

"What can I do?" is a good question. A great offer is, "I can do A, B, or C. Let me know the priority." @utpalvaishnav

_____

_____

_____

128

If your Scrum project did not bring the intended business results, consider mentoring the Product Owner.
@utpalvaishnav

129

In your eyes, if great = good, then it is very unlikely you'll produce great results.
@utpalvaishnav

130

A Scrum team stops learning when it starts believing that it is made of excellent individuals. @utpalvaishnav

_____

_____

_____

131

If you cannot adapt, then what's the point of inspecting? @utpalvaishnav

_____

_____

_____

132

A sprint review is not an approval meeting. Genuine feedback makes the sprint review exercise worthwhile. @utpalvaishnav

_____

_____

_____

133

If you set an agenda for sprint review meetings, you're using Scrum the wrong way. @utpalvaishnav

_____

_____

_____

134

If you love to live with problems and don't want to solve them, Scrum is not for you. @utpalvaishnav

_____

_____

_____

135

Observing from the same lens is important.
Therefore, a co-location is important.
(Virtual co-locations are fine.)
@utpalvaishnav

_____

_____

_____

136

If you have a habit of ending meetings without clear action items, you are most likely going to fail in Scrum.
@utpalvaishnav

137

Email is the last tool that works in Scrum; face-to-face meetings are the best.
@utpalvaishnav

138

If you're pushing any work items onto the team members, you're using Scrum the wrong way. @utpalvaishnav

_____

_____

_____

139

When it comes to Scrum, don't rule out informal meeting spaces (e.g. lunch rooms). Collaboration matters, not the space. @utpalvaishnav

_____

_____

_____

140

A formula good ScrumMasters should follow for identifying impediments: observe, ask, and listen. @utpalvaishnav

_____

_____

_____

About the Author

Utpal "UV" Vaishnav is a lifelong learner and entrepreneur based in Ahmedabad, India.

UV is the co-founder and CEO of Space-O Digicom, a mobile app consulting and product development studio that favors UX over Engineering.

He is also the co-founder of Yories, a personalized storytelling platform for children.

UV consults and mentors startups on bringing their product ideas to life.

Prior to entering the startup world, he facilitated creating software apps and products in various roles ranging from a Software Developer to a Business Unit Head. Agile (especially Scrum) has been his preferred tool of choice throughout the years.

UV writes about his Agile and Scrum experience on www.scrumzen.com.

He blogs at www.utpal.me and tweets as @utpalvaishnav.

AHAthat makes it easy to share, author, and promote content. There are over 30,000 quotes (AHAmessages™) by thought leaders from around the world that you can share in seconds for free.

For those that want to author their own book, we have time-tested proven processes that allow you to write your AHAbook™ of 140 digestible, bite-sized morsels in 8 hours or less. Once your content is on AHAthat, you have a customized url that you can use to have your fans/advocates share your content and help grow your network.

⮑ Start sharing: http://AHAthat.com

⮑ Start authoring: http://AHAthat.com/author

Please pick up a copy of this book in AHAthat and share each AHAmessage socially at http://aha.pub/scrum.

Send an email to hello@utpal.me and write in the subject line: "Scrum Career Question" and ask questions about how Scrum can help you excel in your career. In addition to the free answer to your question, you will also receive a *FREE* copy of my ebook "Build a Winning Career With Scrum" ($6.99 value), where I have written about what it takes to be a Scrum Team Member, ScrumMaster, or a Product Owner. To learn more, please visit www.utpal.me/scrumcareer.

www.ingramcontent.com/pod-product-compliance
Lightning Source LLC
Chambersburg PA
CBHW052147070326
40689CB00050B/2447